Celia Thaxter
An Anthology in Memoriam (1835-1894)

Edited By M. Myers

CELIA THAXTER
An Anthology in Memoriam (1835-1894)

Edited by M. Myers

The cover illustration of Celia Thaxter has been done for the Memorial Anthology of Poetry Series by local artist, Wendy Jo Martin, Elkhart, Indiana. A freelance artist with a portfolio of art with national recognition and acclaim. Her specialties include: signs, murals, window painting, sculpture, logos, set design and scenic painting for T.V., film and stage. A sample of her work can be seen in the movie "Prancer".

Bristol Banner Books
P.O. Box 1219
Bristol, IN 46507

Proofread by Marci Westreich

Library of Congress Catalog Card Number

93-074631

ISBN 1-879183-23-4 paperback

APPRECIATION

Celia Laighton Thaxter was born in Portsmouth, N.H., June 29, 1835 and died in Appledore Island on August 26, 1894. She was the daughter of Thomas B. and Eliza (Rymes) Laighton. Her father was an editor for *New-Hampshire Gazette*, and a member of the state legislature. His family is a descendant of one of the oldest Portsmouth families. He was the keeper of the lighthouse on the Isles of Shoals, and lived in the keeper's cottage on White Island, with his wife and children.

Celia got most of her education from her parents and visitors such as John Weiss and Levi Lincoln Thaxter.

In 1848 Mr. Laighton opened a summer hotel on Appledore Island. Many visitors were attracted to the hotel such as Lowell and Henry David Thoreau. The hotel became a summer haunt for artists and men of letters. Regular visitors to the hotel became close friends of the Laightons. Among them were Whittier the poet and painters William Morris Hunt and Childe Hassam.

After spending two winters at the Shoals, Mr. Thaxter fell in love with his pupil, Ceila Laighton. They got married at Appledore on September 30, 1851. They lived with her family while her husband occupied himself with the pastoral care of the fisher-folk on Star Island. He also studied Browning's poetry, which was his lifelong passion. They had three sons and the oldest was a mental defective and required his mother's care for the remainder of her life. Around 1860 the Thaxters moved to Newtonville, Mass. Mrs. Thaxter pined for the sea and a poem expressing her homesickness titled "Land-Locked", appeared in the *Atlantic Monthly* without her knowledge. The poem had reached Lowell through a friend of hers in which it got published. After being published Mrs. Thaxter was a contributor of poems, sketches and children's stories to various magazines. Her first volume, *Poems* (1872), followed by the notable prose sketches called *Among the Isles of Shoals* (1873), in which it appeared serially in *Atlantic*. Later came *Drift-Weed* (1879), *Poems for Children* (1884), *Edyls and Pastorals* (1886), and *An Island Garden* (1894), illustrations by Childe Hassam.

In 1866 Mrs. Thaxter came back to Appledore to care for her mother after her father died. Her two brothers continued to manage the hotel after her mother died in 1877. Mrs. Thaxter had a cottage nearby where she lived for part of each year. Her many friends appreciated her poetry, painting, and her deep passion for music. The Thaxters moved to Kittery Point, Me. in the autumn of 1880, the same year she visited Europe. There she met Robert Browning and indulged herself in a long rapture of pictures-galleries and concerts. After going home she spent a quiet literary life at Shoals in the summer and the winters in Boston or Portsmouth. Her husband died in 1884 and ten years later Mrs. Thaxter died suddenly at Appledore and was buried there. A year after her death a selection from her letters, *Letters of Celia Thaxter*, was edited by her friends Annie Adams Fields and Rose Lamb, who also prepared the final edition of her *Poems* (1896).

WORKS CITED

Dictionary of American Biography

ON THE PORCH

Where are all the people
Who rocked away the many hours
Watching the front path for glimpses of faces
Of those stopping to say hello

How many lives have been intertwined
With stories told and retold on the porch of time

The soft summer breeze has gently lulled them to doze
Peaceful, quiet, nodding heads, a few muffled snores
Only to be awakened by the cool chill of dusk

Shawls, blankets, bonnets, brimmers
Like soldiers they sit, guarding their sanctuary

Lives that have been full of laughter, tears, happiness, heartaches
Memory retains all to bring comfort and solace
In the approaching winter of their lives

Each rocker to be filled by yet another being
Who will bring new tales of long ago

Oh, the comfort of the rocking chair!
Oh, the pleasure of memories!
Oh, the warmth of sunshine in the twilight years!

Angie Alberico
Erie, PA

OVERSEEING MY AUCTION

Lightly as a moth, my spirit hovers nearby
while the auctioneer
scatters my beloved treasures.
The walnut sideboard,
brought here by wagon so long ago,
is the first thing to be sold.
An expert in antiques knew its worth.
Will she recognize the lingering scent
of ginger cookies and lemon pies;
of cedar oil hand-rubbed into its grain?

Grandmother's low rocking chair
quickly goes for half its value.
The heirloom silver brings a good price.
But who will buy a ragged family album;
A blue, silk wedding garter,
gossamer scraps of handmade lace,
yellowed baby dresses?

"Going -- going," a lifetime's hoard
is so swiftly gone.
Handle my treasures gently, Sojourners,
for the little time you may have
to call them yours.
For you cannot take them with you,
either...

Helen Thomas Allison
Memphis, TN

REPEAT OF WAR

Blind people fighting blind people
A body here
       there
Getting
    deeper
    deeper
       into sleep with every bullet
           slaying
Nature taking a blow
        with every disorder
Awake
    oh
      you fools
        to the beauty
          of your
            soul
        to the Universal Love
           beckoning
           to you
Listen to Its Voice
        so rarely roused

        You veiled its sound
        with your wretched mishmosh
Ah
  to be tempted once more
          by this Voice
  Were I but a fool
        who didn't listen
           now
            ponder
            silently.

Joyce Joyce Andrea
N.Y.C., NY

IN THE SPRINGINNING

Dearest April, tarry some
  I loathe to have you part
Your kisses and your half 'a smile
  Have torn away my heart!

Your promises and little hints
  Delight... so please don't go
Dearest April, tarry awhile
  I'll miss you so, you know.

Small pilgrim and life's lover
  Retard not your gaze
On my simple beauty
  I must needs be on my way

Else meadows and spring's verdure
  Be bereft of noonday's shade
And the light of torrid sun
  Be too much for mortal's gaze.

And so we embraced, and April
  Touched by our discourse
Shed many great and cooling tears
  Of sadness and remorse

Bringing land her fertile beauty
  Washing, cleansing all the earth.
Good-bye now, till next spring
  Till once we'll meet again.

Yes, I am coming soon!
MARANATHA
Come Lord Jesus! COME

Sister Mary Regina of the Angels
West Springfield, MA

EARTH

Cradle this Earth, Father, as she heaves in grief.
Slashed and scarred as Hate bounces off her belly.
Battered by winds stripping her forests bare to frozen twigs;
Her hillsides, rain-drenched, sliding into the crashing sea.

In love You created her and set Your people upon her.
Man and Woman and Beast shared the Green Peace
With You. Nothing to lack. Rocks breathing Your care.

Tumultuous Hate, scorching Envy, Arrogance fire-fed.
Would this Earth could turn Sin back into deserted Time;
To forever disappear.

Bette Armstrong
Overland Park, KS

THE PHOTOGRAPH

We study a black and white photo --
children dressed in white
dancing in a graveyard,

mass-produced markers battleship gray
lined up like left-right, left-right
feet of war.

There is a precise spacing between souls.
Charcoal trees drip intermezzo rain,
the sky -- a blind mute -- stares.

Headstones converge like spent arrows
on dull dark grass,
but seven carefree kids

in almond-tree white
hands joined
circle and sing as they dance.

Claire J. Baker
San Pablo, CA

NO BOOHOOING

When I lie there for viewing
Let laughter fill the room
No sadness, tears, nor rueing
No harbingers of gloom

While I lie there for viewing
Let's pray, then sing a song
I'll be watching what you're doing,
I'll be there to sing along.

My spirit will be soaring
So, no sadness here below
Like the ocean roaring,
Drown out all tears and woe.

As I lie there, dead and cold,
Don't think about my body,
Just know my spirit's brave and bold
And nothing will be shoddy.

When I lie there for viewing,
Just hum a prayer or two-
Let there be no boohooing
Cause I'll be with 'you know who'.

Dorothy M. Barkin
Pittsburgh, PA

8 SEPTEMBER

At Jenny Handel's Memorial Service
The cantor read that we are like grass
Growing and withering.

At Jenny Handel's memorial Service
Her friend said that
After Jenny defended her brothers once in school
And became scratched up herself,
Jenny said: "What do you do when
They are beating up your brothers."

It was said that
For a few years Jenny and her husband
Moved from place to place
In a gypsy like existence.

It was read that
Jenny was like a woman
Of valor and a woman of kindness.

It was said that
Jenny found her home in Santa Barbara.

At Jenny Handel's Memorial Service
The cantor sang
In the Memorial Prayer
That Jenny would have
Rest, eternity, refuge, and an inheritance of God.

After Jenny Handel's Memorial Service
And her body had been laid to rest,
A train passed by Jenny and
Her kindred souls, resting in
Parched green hills below the western slope.

Merle Ray Beckwith
Santa Barbara, CA

ONCE AND FUTURE KINGDOM

Too few Galahads,
Suffering our scorn
As quixotic buffoons,
While Modreds slurp the limelight,
Hogging center stage.

All Lancelots are gridlocked.
Their dilemmas abound and bind.
Guineveres are seduced, bribed or raped--
No Almesbury sanctuary
To be had for love or money.

A plethora of Merlin's handiwork
Without the wizard's wisdom--
Apprentices still tinker and tamper.
Their mentor yet entwined, so
Chaos emerges by the Lady of the Lake.

Arthur come forth from Avalon!
Resurrect the clean cuts of Excalibur,
The chivalrous chime, the round table right.
Morgana must not hold you entombed
While Camelot's remnants crumble.

Richard F. Bell
Marquette, MI

RESURGENT WAVE

It was an ideal day at the beach for one,
little superior to a common grain of sand,
a bronzed withered walking tomb,
the resting place of forgotten ideals,
little learned, little known.
The one vanished into a frothy sea of fools
without recourse, only to be resurrected
into the amorphous mass of the faceless mortals
to join in festive mood of ignorance.

Robert S. Blake
North Haven, CT

FORTITUDE

A blanched rose, tender to the touch,
became pinkish at petals' edge
within the light of brighter days,
its cup started to open wide
in state of want for spring nectar.

The sap was building all day long
anticipating bee's contact;
the hours passed, the dusk appeared
and petals felt a coming frost;
in passing wind, the rose withstands.

Emma J. Blanch
Milford, CT

WINTER

Mom fell on the ice today
An ambulance came and took her away
With a blank stare
The flashing lights eased my pain
But hers still exists
Whenever they predict freezing rain.

Nicole Borelli
Bensalem, PA

BORNE WITH THE SPIRIT

The wind blows where it will
The mighty rush you hear
leap heart - with worship fill
that once was beatless - drear.

Come tongues of fire
and rest on us
the sleeping dust
awake - inspire.

Whence sprung this Spirit God
this gusty whip of wind
restoring thirsty pod
so streams of life begin?

Come tongues of fire
and rest on us
the sleeping dust
awake - inspire.

Whither this Spirit goes
mystery beyond our ken
one deep to the other knows
praising with loud amen.

Betsy J. Bramhall
Morristown, NJ

=30

12, 13, 16, 18, 21, 42
follow me, know me, live with me

such change delights us
oaks replace the times
not always to our liking perhaps

the deer we knew for years are no longer there
the lack of human comfort
almost completely in the past
often more difficult than it might appear

nature has no guile
bends north toward provincetown
into some great abyss
many large glacial boulders

lichened, poorly soiled
giving precisely the wrong impression
my wild neighbors
sibble me, me you
without which we die

wet, black eyes
suddenly bolting, knowing where and who they are
I stop, surrounded surrounded in silence
no entrance, however much craved; only only passage

this is something in the nature of a confession, I suppose
but: of what?
and you, you listener? voyeur. part the crown the crowd of cars

in rebuke of the first person singular

David Branco
Fairhaven, MA

VOCATIONAL CHANGE

Midway through this life, with difficulty overcoming me,
I found myself forced to change my course.
All which had given joy and gladness left
As I felt the surge of incompleteness flood
Upon all of my best laid plans and fondest hopes.
No longer would my childish ways secure the future;
Nor would their weaknesses vanish with them.
Instead I would have to pay the price.
The price of returning to my earliest days
With a whip of cruel thongs
To thrash out the remaining life of ghosts
Once most powerful and in control;
Now retaining only their ability to frighten
And to threaten my commitment to change.

John Britt
Dayton, OH

MAGIC MOTION
(Ruby-throated humming bird)

A sonant presence targets floral bells;
It hovers as it sips - its wings a blur
Of animated prisms - then repels
A bold intruder in a skyward whir.
These birds that upthrust and reverse with ease,
Have speeds to execute at their command
Maneuvers which defy analyses -
Are miniature jewels from fairyland.

A welcome does not always come in words;
Mine manifests in baskets hung with bloom
And feeders, nectar filled, to greet these birds,
Whene'er their summer sojourn they resume.
I sense that magic overflows my cup
When ruby-throated hummers come to sup.

Rose Winters Burns
N.S., Canada

MITZY (from this angle)

With poisonous bangles
And delicate dreams
She moves through my soul like venom
And into my heart with ease
Love must sting, she believes
No reply
No reply
Her dark eyes hold me still
With half-truths
And rest for the weary
Decked out in barbed wire and glittering gold
She separates man from myth and reaches out
As I reach in
Our fingertips touch and worlds collide
From right to left
Her skin reads like a parable
Told by a wanderer
Her years are centuries
Her nights are stolen
And I, with my time at hand
Talk to the night and wonder how
She has learned to console the beast
To tame the wolf
When love is legendary
And as her grip tightens
I feel myself come apart
I feel the walls close in
I feel the struggle mount
And I know that between Heaven and Hell
There is no place like her
No place
At all

Howard Camner
Miami, FL

STRAIGHTSHOOTING

And then it was July 4th in Athens, Georgia. It is
always July 4th in Athens, even though today is only the
2nd. If I were a good writer like everyone says James
Joyce is, it would all mean something. But it doesn't.
It's all lies, so don't believe anything. I'm not Joyce,
but if we're lucky, I'll tell some of my lies pretty enough,
lies such as my lovers or best friends tell, and if we
wish hard and cross our fingers, click our heels three
times Dorothylike of the ruby slippers, they'll all come
true. Oh I am a writer who has no writing, so now, look,
printed words upon a page. I have been practicing though,
lying, that is, reciting my lies all in my head. Big lies,
small lies, nice ones, mean ones, lies enough to fill a hole
in my head. Tell me a lie. I'll tell you some - I'll tell
you what you want to hear. All lies. I'll tell you what.
Since we're friends, I'll tell you some of my best whoppers,
and we'll see what you think. I've practiced, and now I
want to share the lies that have given me the most pleasure.

And then it was July 4th in Athens, Georgia. The sky
went snap crackle pop as vast watermelons descended from
heaven to suckle the patriot horde. Oh you held my hand
and said you loved me. I knew you meant it and hugged you
as fried chicken, potato salad and cole slaw flowed out
from beneath the baseball bleachers. Sweat was in the winds
and cotton candy rained down as eagle feathers and red, white,
blue confetti for one nation under God. And did you know?
Christ was never murdered, the Titanic never sank, Camelot
never fell and you'll always be so good to me, kind and
caring as the comely Pooh Bear could ever be. And you know
what? I cannot tell a lie.

Wil Carter
East Point, GA

CAT'S-EYES

Wayward wings that ride on the wind,
Leaves that cling to the trees, lover rescue me,
For night is coming, shadows that prevail.
Trains crashing, broken bodies on the six o'clock news,
We don't need their pain, we revel in Eden,
Tiny critters come out to meet us, they see love's glow,
Nothing to fear, the sunlight silhouette of bees floating over sunflowers.
Holding hands, walking towards the sunrise with hope,
That this world can come together, make all the right moves,
Learn from the mistakes everything that history proves.
We glide across silver lakes, like bright angels floating on a breeze,
Running in the rain, love hearts on the oaktree, Kensington Park,
Fingers that sign write love poems across the pale blue skies,
This linear dream swirls through time, behind the image of her diamond eyes.
Beauty that spellbounds, cat's-eyes, make you laugh and cry,
Corridors and passages, infinity at the end of her halls of fame,
The apocalypse of my duality, I wish to play love's game.

Glenn Cavanagh
Queensland, Australia

LITTLE SISTER

I watched you grow from A to Z,
I laughed when you would imitate me.

I watched you grow from the tiniest flower,
And before I knew, it was your wedding shower.

I watched in amazement the beautiful bride,
Walk down the isle with such grace and pride.

Now the news of a baby that you've told,
Has thrilled me more then a pot of gold.

I watched every scene of your life as it grew,
Now my biggest dream is to imitate you!

Dedicated to Michele Angela,
Love,   Pappy   XO

Patricia Lynn Cisco
Wenonah, NJ

SYLVESTER'S BALLAD

Why write about a cartoon character?
Faute de mieux
Watching Saturday morning entertainment
At seven years while I ate chocolate-
covered grahams looking forward to
An entire summer of no school

A gathering of youth watched and
Laughed, adults as well, a tribute
To the futility of your feline edacity
As you expectorated on the celluloid
Walt was humbled I'm certain
You should consider yourself lucky
They laugh at me in the desert
Write one about me.

> Your greatest fan,
> Sincerely
> Wyle Coyote

> Stephen Clements
> Binghamton, NY

THAT MADE EARTH

At the tail end of the Rockies
in the Big Bend of West Texas
you can feel
the movement of
pools of air
in the world's spine,
lowest source of mentation
the movement of first chacra
starting to
work its
way
up.

I can feel the source of air
humming
up the cord
illera
deep in
mantle.

The white hot magma
that made mountains
that made plains
that made Earth.

Jim Cody
El Paso, TX

LOVING CARE—EVERYWHERE

"Dear Lord, I pray that You will be
near to those who need you most.
Whether they be close to home
or on Asia's rocky coast.
Sooth them with Your Spirit Lord;
please help them realize,
they couldn't be in better hands.
You are loving, gentle and wise.

I know, while You care for needy ones
You still remain close to me.
How You accomplish the good You do
in each life is a mystery.
Faith holds the key to many doors,
and if one's faith be strong.
They may sense Your Presence where'er
they go,
though the journey be oh, so long."

God is not bound by strands of steel
or tossed by winds that blow.
His strength is like a gentle breeze,
which calms the troubled soul.
When you feel the need of your Father's love.
Have faith, He will be right there.
No matter how far you chance to stray,
He will keep you in His care.

Patti Cordell
Flora Vista, NM

APRIL SNOW RAGA

Snow falls on an early April morning, rain falls
all day, on snow, grass, on red buds swelling
on grey branches, as small green buds burst:

your Brookine library card checks out 5 discs;
you fill this rainy afternoon listening to
Piatigorsky premier Walton's cello concerto

while radiator waves rise thru the tabletop
as you type; the record disconnects; you pause;
age: 32, occupation: writer, income: unemployment.

you've left apprenticeship; you've lost intensity
& pleasure in what you write: it comes easier,
goes easier, like this loose rage; you know

you're writing to be read by others, you're
no longer improvising on typewriter pages
or moving your pentel pen across the pad

as April rain melts early April snow, you
write, tensionlessly as Vaughan Williams'
3rd Symphony's concentrics rise, you write

unplanned, unexpected, unresisted triolets
building to climax, watermarking your poems
with coda, chorale, struck chordal variants,

while Margaret Ritchie's off-stage cantilena
dissolves into its final moderato maestoso,
as April rain dissolves April snow

Bill Costley
Wellesley, MA

TREASURE DRAWER

A drawer in Grandmother's kitchen
Filled with "treasures" mostly old
Gave us hours of fun perusing
Items with histories yet untold.

Nuts and bolts and twine and string,
Corks, checkers and marbles by the score,
Doorknobs and a brass-plated hinge,
Golf balls aplenty, some nude to the core.

Skate keys, balls of foil and yo yo's,
Rubber bands and tops of jars,
Plain spoons, sugar shells and seashells,
Paper wrappers and boxes for cigars.

Keys no longer with locks to open,
Banks once used for storing coins,
Collar buttons, chains and buckles,
Handles, jacks and napkin rings.

Screwdrivers, rulers, tape measure and rope,
A cowbell, wax candles, some washers, a belt,
Measuring spoons and clothespins, a spring for a clock,
A doorknocker, buttons and pin cushion of felt.

Our attention was focused on items galore;
We'd play by the hour, my brother and I
In that drawer full of "treasures" in Grandmother's kitchen,
In those days so long gone by.

Shoelaces, button hook, an earring of pearl,
Parts of a lantern, an old rusty spike,
A bookmark with Biblical words on the front,
A clip for one's ankle when riding a bike.

It held our attention for hours on end...
That drawer full of "treasures" to touch and to see,
In Grandmother's kitchen we loved so much...
Those wonderful "toys" for my brother and me.

Phyllis Crago
Prairie Village, KS

IN THE COURSE OF TIME EVERYONE IS A POET

Collapse--in the way of strings snapping;
And no wings to convey alone or ever:
That it happened before on a screen
Beyond a childhood gaze, knowing it
In variegated sorrow;--mid self
Placating stanzas at a price--though
Linked with the great puzzle of the
One--see it in the white clothes, injury
And paradise, coded in a book for the
Little, with artists' hands, full of
Longing. The heart is rising and one knows
The bounty: and though these days unroll
And wait, one is off-balance seeing no
Secret in which to grow old--hands
Ungrasped which once feared their burden--
Unseen, misunderstood--waiting among
Unpleasant fugitive nights, where
"This you do" while growing out of the
Season to die are flowers left whole
In the massacre, leading a welcome wound
From the bitter dislocation of wandering
Away, not knowing from what, (usually
Places near what could be if life ever
Rested from the harrying wind beating
Down poets from a true heritage) to the
Assured love found in letters that wait
To be written--opening others like them,
Like moments that waited for you.

Arthur Croe
Niagara Falls, NY

THE LAST FAREWELL

Perhaps in Heaven
the dandelions never wilt
and my friend, the sandpiper,
will greet me at the Door
and I will work again
  in a garden
and smell again
  the fresh salt spray
and see at night
  the starry skies
and look down on my son
with his love of plants
  and nature
but I have my doubts.
I want to linger on
enjoying Earth's
  special pleasures--
But I must go.

Mary Louise Curtis
Pensacola, FL

THE ROOSTER AND THE HEN

The Rooster struts
pretentiously
thinking he owns the Hen
But she owns he
for without her
he's just another sound
at sunrise

The Hen sets
complacently
thinking she owns the Rooster
(for without her, he
is just another sound at sunrise)
But he owns she
for without him
she only lays
omelets for breakfast

Jeff Custer
San Pablo, CA

IT IS ALL I ASK

Please don't ever smile for me,
Don't even look my way.

For in your heart there's no love for me,
Your heart I cannot sway.

Just an empty shell remains
Of the girl I used to be.

No living, vibrant person exists
She died with your love for me.

To have you turn away
Was more than I could bear.

So, please don't ever smile for me,
For I'm no longer there.

Julia A. David
West Middlesex, PA

OPERA SINGER AND THE TIGHTROPE WALKER

Above the arena
amid rocketing
lights, the tightrope
walker toeholds
with balance pole
knowing
an audience
breathes
for the conquering
of that space.

In the theatre
after the opening
prelude
an opera singer
glides
on pageantry
of tones aware
music lovers
listen
for the quavering
vibration
of a note.
What cannot be known
remains the unseen
calisthenics
of an artist's soul.

Irene Dayton
East Flat Rock, NC

GENTLE RAIN

Gentle rain, soaking the earth
Buds open thirsty for the raindrops,
The grass clean and shiny is more
green than ever.
What marvel is the rain, Lord,
How about a like shower of graces,
  We thirst.

Persons on drugs would turn with
sudden surprise
at Your grace-shower,
Young women with new-eyes would look
upon "life" as shared creation.
Addicts would steady their wobbly
determination.
We, ourselves would take a step
closer to You, Lord.
  We thirst.

S. June Desmond
Fond du Lac, WI

MOON POEM

Listen: talk to me. Draw for me, if you will,
Everything you can think of personally
On the moon, documentary or symbolic. I know
Next to nothing, only a few things
About that yellow cruiser up there.

Look, how that loyal sweetheart seems to hang out--
Evidence that you can't always go
On what your eyes report to your mind.
No, it's not just hanging there but cruising
Along with this our earth, over the Ranchos Church.

Love and the earth are properly synonymous in
Eternal terms, and even in the short term
Often enough for somebody like myself.
Now wouldn't that mean love modulates
About fifty-six thousand miles an hour, and that

Love, like the earth, characteristically moves so
Exquisitely fast that it seems to loaf?
Okay, okay, I've spun far out off the point.
Now tell me what you know about the "harvest" moon
And a "strawberry" moon--things like that, if you will.

R. P. Dickey
Ranchos de Taos, NM

VISITORS

Familiar clucking sounds
Outside the window
Orange breasted robins
Skimming across the lawn
Listening for worms
Before flying north
Bringing memories of home.

Bettina B. Dietrich
Madison, FL

AT LEAST THE END WAS PEACEFUL

those fifteen years
won't be forgotten
never to be thought of in vain
so loyal and so true
i can't stop loving you
pain came your way
now it's ended
am i selfish to feel this way?
you were honest you were good
my heart will always long for you
i can't see straight
nothing could ever replace
this empty feeling inside
i wish i could be there where you are
we could be so happy
i guess it's good, in a way
you're probably running and playing
like you used to
God it hurts so bad
i really miss you

Jennifer Dopkin
Richboro, PA

LETTER OF THANKS TO THE INCOMPARABLE DOCTOR BROTHER BODHISATTVA MEHRDAD MASSOUDI

On this freezing cold night the wind has come up
howling from the lands of the hordes, and the snow
is piled higher than the doors and windows of this
pitiful log house, but I want you to know
  I am warm inside the lamb's wool sweater
your mother made with her delicate Persian
hands--the great white sweater with the strong
shoulders and the corded braids across the chest

  --a temple of a sweater, or a pale forest
of a thousand trees--the distinguished white
sweater made with the eight intelligent white
buttons--the brave sweater I am wearing on this
freezing cold night as I fearlessly gallop
across the desert, I am laughing at the spears
and arrows of innumerable Philistine foul
winded armies of lies, deceit and cultural
decrepitude--because I am wearing the invincible
sweater of no defeat or surrender

  made by the hundred hands of the kindest
woman for her straight-backed strong-hearted
son--named after the great Persian king, whose
status I somehow share inside this soft Persian
  ocean of place and time. On this freezing cold
night, I am warm--even as I write to you--even
as I remain, sincerely, faithfully, your brother
always, as you have always faithfully remained mine.

J. C. Ellefson
Middlebury, VT

EVENING SNOWFALL

Sounds of rush hour
duel to twinkling lights,
barbs on fence
turn into fluff balls,
the meeting of another
is enveloped in soft greeting.
Nature's comforter.

Margaret English
Novato, CA

WINTER THEME

save
the last breath
of a cold and merciless winter
a reign of shapeless icicles
the snowy empire and freezing fingers
of death on lifeless carcasses
frost-bitten but well preserved
the cycle of nature in all its magnificence
annihilated by
technological creations badly utilised
by man
his lust
and ambition for the scientific quest
the far away sound
of bells chiming
a requiem
as a funeral cortege
silently skirted
through deoxygenised
air

R. Fenech
Malta G. C., Europe

SEAN

Sleeping in the silence of the night,
So still and peaceful,
With the cares of the day
Behind him.

Then, as morning light
Enters the room,
He awakens
As a new day dawns.

Soon he becomes aware of the time,
And all senses come alive.
Such energy emerges, ebbing and flowing
During the coming hours.

Everything is new and waiting to be explored.
Inside, imagination reigns.
A table becomes a car,
A chair turns into a sleigh.

Then crayons are used
To create special reflections,
Left to imagery
That only a child understands.

Soon the day will come to an end,
Bringing new adventures
On the morrow.

Karen A. Flynn
Pittsburgh, PA

ON LINE

I've been on a two month drunk to the moon and stars,
want to sleep for a week while someone does my laundry,
pull the down comforter up, tight to my chin,
hide out until my classes start again.

Oh, the things I have seen and dreamt this while,
of the gods descended to a handy star,
ambrosial nectar singing in purple veins,
the star the star of wisest men and women.

I see she came on strong while you were manic,
says June Nelle, with the kindness of a lifetime.
You need quiet and a rest before
you start again, all the pressure off.

Check your lithium level quite carefully,
says Daisy, but you were right on the mark:
God is being quite sadly churlish these days.
"'Missing the target,' 'off the mark' is 'sin,'"

the Bible says. I was on line for these
two months, at the bull's eye. Too bad I was high,
the ancient gods were just fooling around,
the dawn was dawning in the troubled west.

Leslie D. Foster
Marquette, MI

PEGASUS ON WHEELS

Transported over the macadam,
In our zephyrous automobile,
We rein a fiery chariot,
Impelled by horses volatile.

We sped toward future horizons,
From the cares of the past afar;
The present nonlimited
By the confines of the car.

Our Father's creation
Unreels swiftly before us:
The restful plantation,
The inspiring forest.

The artifacts of man
Now dart beyond our fenders:
Here billboards incongruent,
There telephone-wired timbers.

We sway our circular sceptre
As sovereigns over the highway,
Yet mindful Damoclean Death
Controls each pass and byway.

Along the asphalt flying,
Astride our wingéd roan,
We foretaste the celerity
of Cherubs and of Throne.

We must at length descend to earth
From our Elysian mirage;
We welcome standstill hearth and berth,
Corral our steed in the garage.

Sr. Mary Lawrence Franklin
Erie, PA

GROUND HOG DAY
(A Painting By Andrew Wyeth)

From the corner kitchen window
Splashed with sun,
Karl Kuerner's single placed
Noon-time table setting
Backdrops the ax-chipped logs
Of the gumwood tree
That represent his day's labor.

Log chains are yet wrapped
Round one girth,
The sections, team skidded
From near the pasture pond;

The logs and solitary
Fence post cast their mythic
Shadow to confine
The ground hog, but not Karl,
To another six week hibernation.
The Spring farm work will go on.

Lee Frisbee
Brockport, NY

LET'S TALK

How can you hate someone you don't even know
This I will never grasp
I try to come up with reasons, I try to think it through
There are so many questions to be asked
You've never even met me
You don't even know my name
So how come you've already judged me
And have placed on me the blame
How come you're pointing your finger
How come you're turning away
I haven't even spoken a word
But then what is there to say
It seems you have ideas, already your mind is set
You didn't give me the chance to make my impression yet
I guess you've already decided
That there's something wrong with me
Although we haven't even explored
Friendship as a possibility
Were you taught these feelings
Or did you have a choice
Is it because of where I come from
My eyes, my skin, my voice
There is still time to change
If you are willing to try
To open up your ears, your heart
To open up your eyes
Sometimes I want to scream at you
To hurt you deep inside
To make you feel like you want me to
To diminish all your pride
But sometimes I just want to talk
To listen to your reasons
That we may somehow open a door
For all the ages to come

Christina Frondoso
Irvine, CA

LIFE RETURNS

Oh little leaf
from bud you grow,
on mother's arms
in the breeze you blow.

You grow and nurture
with the daylight sun,
the wind and rain
your playground fun.

Many brothers and sisters
there will be,
mother will be proud
that giant tree.

Many will watch
at your colors bright,
they contrast the beauty
of the sky so light.

When you fall through the air
don't ever fear,
mother is there watching
no need for a tear.

When lying on the ground
so damp and cold,
never let make you feel
like you are old.

Over the long winter
your snow blanket heats,
all of God's blessings
at mother's feet.

In the beauty and brightness
of the new found spring,
you will be back little leaf
a brand new thing.

Kenneth Gadke
Cleveland, OH

IN THE EYE OF RADIANCE
(for Gertrude Ryder Bennett)

I see you in a bower of words,
honeysuckle and yellow roses.
I see you in sun and lilting shade,
hands outstretched,
learning, understanding, accepting,
and always, through gently falling days,
sharing fragrance from your garden.

Joan Austin Geier
Roosevelt Island, NY

TOUCHING HIS LIMITS

The stars, so far
Remote and unattainable
The dreams, so fragile,
Often vain; but man
With spirit indomitable
Surges forward
Touching his limits
Blossoms where he stands.

Helen B. Glass
Rancho Cordova, CA

SNAPSHOT OF SUMMER

I marvel at survival! Summer sound
Recurring each new season strikes a chord.
shoots from refurbished roots surmount the ground
In self-set images, all looking toward
Fulfillment of tradition, form and face.
The feisty dandelion will uphold -
Be it unwelcome - its accustomed place,
And meadow buttercups their soft touch gold.

"Love me not" non-stop daisy petals will
In breezeless silence, even, clockwise bend,
Till birdwing song breaks on the clovered still
With jarring note of an approaching end.
In flick of flash a flaming landscape and
September holding summer in one hand!

Hazel Firth Goddard
Dartmouth, Canada

A SONNET
(In Memory of Celia Laighton Thaxter)

Oh, what a woman, a gem of many facets!
As John Alsbee wrote in tribute to Celia,
His neighbor more than a hundred years ago,
She was equally at home in the kitchen,
With spade and trowel in her garden,
With poets, artists, sailors, scholars, and children.
No way did he suspect her hatred of the kitchen,
Her longing for more time for her poetry and art.

And yet she left us such a heritage of
Poems rich in imagery and warmth and
Memorable lines: "Love shall save us all" and
"The sunrise never failed us yet."
Are we not God's children both, Celia, you and I
As I neglect the evening meal to write a poem?

Emma Leigh Goodwin
Upper Nyack, NY

THE SUBSTITUTE

Her clouded mind keeps wandering back
When she tucked her brood in bed
Except the youngest one, the babe,
First must be changed and fed

She lulled her in her rocking chair
She hugged her from all harm
She felt so needed, useful then,
Her world was right and warm

Her brood grew up and went away
Her home now one for "olds"
While in her wheelchair every day
A well-worn doll she holds

Other "live-ins" dot the halls
She doesn't seem to see
She hugs the doll as nurses pass
Content in reverie

Where are the ones she lulled to sleep
You never see them there
They're all successful but so sad
They have no time to spare

She must now wait for her reward
In a far better sphere
She can leave behind the "comfort doll"
It won't be needed here....................

Helen A. Gougeon
Florence, MA

LAMPLIGHT

```
        around my
   rs            la
    te           mp,
   ut
 fl               bu
                   lb


  th                 du
Mo                   st
      on  my  papers.
       Wind from
       the balcony,
        my body
        a chunk.
       My head
         cruel
       I stare
       down into
       the street,
while my soul roves the bridge on the river where fog has risen.
       On the bridge I stare into the mirror-cracked water,
       swaths of fog over it, perhaps the river rising.
              Bat flaps
              by my ear,
               chalklight
                smudges my cheek.
                Wind curls around the
              st                    n.
              re                    ma
               et
               la                    ng
                mp,                  hu
                 long-necked like a
```

Ray Greenblatt
Paoli, PA

SAFE

Hold me; please don't ever let me go.
When I'm with you, I can feel no sorrow.
Nothing comforts me like your warm embrace,
Nothing is as soothing as your gentle face.
In my life, I never really felt safe before,
Now there's you; I don't need anything more!

Devon Grove-Merritt
Dayton, OH

THE CHARTERED COURSE

My footsteps choose a chartered course;
And yet, I seek another realm.
My ship is tossed on stormy seas;
Oh, Lord, is no one at the helm?

I longed to find a tranquil port,
But trials and sorrows found instead;
And so my dreams, like morning mists,
Were quickly scattered as they fled.

And then one day at last I learned,
That peace is found in Him alone.
His Love enfolds my wandering soul,
Secure in Knowing I'm His own.

Connie Guido
Arlington Hts., IL

FOR DIANE

I fold her voice,
put it in a pocket.
Not to have a sheet of music,
but a map of that riverbed
where words thin,
the heart suddenly becomes an ear,
a listening post,
on that vast floe of desire
where our bodies
pitch a tent.

Jim Handlin
Plainfield, NJ

A CASUAL GLANCE

They briefly read the headlines
in the *New York Times,* she realized,
though, that they should prepare
for the day; he arose first,
handing the *Times* to her;
then he threw off his nightshirt,
and entered the bathroom to shower and shave;
she scanned an article, but lost interest,
when she heard the dishes declaring breakfast;
she removed her nightgown, and placed
it on the bed; she hurriedly showered
so she could set the table; newly
christened into the day, they could
share their schedules, and sanctify
their wedding vows once again.

For within a half hour, they'd
write a new biography to share
at tomorrow's breakfast.

Paul A. Hanson
Sheboygan, WI

WINTRY SQUALLS

Howling winds
driving rain,
landscape blurred
fogged windowpane.

Misty suds
roads all wet,
no abating
weather set.

Tall trees twist
bend and sway,
branches snap,
break away.

Lashing hilltop,
shore and sea,
unleashed fury
wild and free.

Paul Haugh
Queensland, Australia

THE CANYON

Time's aged and stony monument
Weathers grain by grain.
What the river's fury left
Now melts in wind and rain.

A thousand shadow fingers reach
Beyond the grand abyss
To touch unconquered cliffs aglow
In sunset's fading kiss.

A nether world of dark and light
Cast in a vision sublime;
A window to the ages
Sealed in the bonds of time.

Behold the ancient rocks
Where primordial fossils trod
And sense the humbleness of man
Before the face of God.

C. David Hay
Rosedale, IN

PINK BOUQUET

Roses pink, growing wild along the creek -
Pink, blending as when pinched my lovers cheek -
Aptly named and divinely new,
When gathered to enjoy, a lovely bouquet for all
   to view -
Feelings and visions and memories are what life
   is all about -
As roses blooming free along the creeks of life,
   silently shout -
Pick them gently, face the wind, and from their capture
   let them out.

Carl D. Haynes
Marion, IN

FIRST SUMMER NIGHT

This was the Night I dreamed about all winter
During those endless dreary dark cold months
When the windows rattled and the furnace ran
The curtains closed in the evening and the quilt on the bed
I thought about the first night the windows would be open
And the summer sounds would drift across the air
The noises from the amusement park
And the impatient horns at the drive-in movie
Traffic noises and people's voices floating up
And I would listen with just a linen sheet covering me
This was the first night and it was wonderful
I endured another winter just to hear a summer night.

Rita M. Herold
Erie, PA

AFTERMATH

a ticket to the end
Bryndy demanded after release
from army service
restrictions and war
it was time to move on
you can have a ticket home
any further you pay more
that you can do on board
no more could be expected
not complaining really
Bryndy said
just testing the system
at first it was crowded
but later Bryndy was alone
in a tunnel drilled through darkness
following the headlight
at the terminus Bryndy faced ahead
towards the flat horizon
with not a backward glance
it was the same all around
but somewhere must be hills
the stumps of Gondwana
the original ancient continent
Bryndy's obsession was to find gold
in a panning dish
perhaps also a nugget
then follow the traces
back to the mother lode
a thick stratum of pure gold
or even a yellow metal road
that was the tale Bryndy told
to allay suspicions
on a personal mission
to discover whatever was
in silence finding serene solace

Bernard Hewitt
Cairns, Australia

AUTUMN REPOSE

On misty, frosty, Autumn morn
When all the earth is still
I love to watch the morning sun
Come rising o'er the hill.

And all the world below responds
To warmth and light above
Makes one so glad to be alive
This time of year we love.

Take in that cool fresh smell of Fall
Whose sweetness you can't match
The fragrance of the ripened corn
And pumpkins in the patch.

This harvest time is just so grand
When sights and smells abound
Enjoy what God is offering now
While Autumn's still around.

Let's take a walk down natures path
Mid foliage of all shades
And see the sights that Fall provides
Mid woodland, hills, and glades.

Stop in beside a roadside stand
And see the harvest store
It's Autumn's bounty at its best
You've not to want for more.

There's apples, pumpkins, squash, and corn
A most colorful display
You'd best come now, October calls
Or you'll wait another day.

For soon twill all be over
And the Winter wind will howl
And we'll praise Him for His blessings
When we partake Thanksgiving fowl.

Walter E. Hire
Middlebury, IN

THE JUDGEMENT OAK

A towering oak once stood within a yard
  Beside a house built of great blocks of stone,
Cut from the cliffs along a mighty stream
  That flows from distant mountains of the west.

That tree became the courthouse for a man,
  Whose pioneering travels brought him here
In later years of life to build that house,
  And hear court cases in its leafy shade.

The ancient tree no longer stands today,
  But by its stump a marker tells the tale,
How Daniel Boone had meted justice there
  Beneath the branches of the Judgement Oak.

Albert R. Horrell
Harvester, MO

2012 A.D.

Lo! Death has joined the Eternal Round
O Dweller of the Earth, another cycle has begun.
The End is the same as the beginning and we are bound
To a little system and one sun.

The Pleiadian Beam has elevated the mists
And transcended the void to glide and wander
Above the Ninth Heaven if it exists,
Gog and Magog, up from under.

We Earthlings cleaned our abodes,
Put out all the pilot lights,
Boarded our boats and rowed
As the solar force field arrived that night.

Some of our idle ones chose to linger
In the back streets to commit
Robbery and murder and point their finger
To their sacrifice and thanksgiving for it.

Others of us mind-torture our loved ones
And count ourselves civilized.
Our message to the Pleiadians remains trivialized:
"Beam us up, please. We wish to become
A part of you. We promise not to sodomize."

From veils of haze now comes the Solar Cycle gleam,
Here strange new latitudes for the poles
While psychic and solar forces stream
And myriad islands, coastlines, snowflakes run
Till, gathered by a force converging,
The sundered filaments are one.

Blind stood the physicist by the roaring sea.
Waves surged round him unendingly,
And the gigantic works of the scientific age
Merged round him with all its pageantry.

Had sight been his, he had seen that day
Heaven and Sea as Earth dissolved away.

Louise Horton
Granger, TX

COMPOSITION IN LATE AUTUMN

dearest darling cut thru my thoughts
beyond cherotic license
a place finite
where everybody is a STAR
and every thing
is an open secret.

speak to me in the most
quiet of places
i need the comfort of yur NO noise
yur pur   fect ecletic
soft/ soft whispers
of unbabylon

yur hands on my face.

Pure delight of the bright dawn
as so many coloured leaves
fractures the tense brilliance
of your grey blue eyes
and becomes
my constant catechism.

There is an incredible softness
in the heart of your movements
a tai chi of the mind:

We touch fingers
and watch the world change

out into
the pure light
of leaves spinning on pavement
as another star
fades quietly
into the white.

Noni Howard
Pacifica, CA

WHO WALK NOT IN THE LIGHT

I really cannot bear his eyes
that look on me accusingly;
yet it was he who chose to drown
in youthful waters long ago:
And thus become a living ghost
who never sees the Holy One
smiling upon us lovingly.
If only I could bring some light
into this dark, diurnal round,
resuscitate his spirit's joy
to contemplate the sweet divine
that permeates our universe:
where humans, like us, fail to tread
beyond the gutters of despair.

Patricia Howe
Irchester, England

REFLECTIONS FOR A WOMAN

As in the days of old you heard
The angry shouts to crucify,
So in these days the women shout
"It is our right. The child must die."

Oh woman, is it legal now
A healthy fetus to abort?
Because our leaders tell us so,
And nine from our *Highest Court?*

Oh woman, who has given them
The right to snuff away a life?
And who has given them the right
To poison, choke, or use a knife?

Oh woman, see the severed limbs,
The knife that stopped a beating heart,
All thrown into a bloody pail,
Then wheeled away upon a cart!

Oh woman, think, the boy you killed.
He could have grown to be a man,
A famous doctor finding cures
For cancer, AIDS, with God he'd plan.

Oh woman, did you ever think
The boy could be your pride and joy?
When all are gone and you're alone
He'd comfort you, "Your little boy?"

Oh woman, when you're old and grey,
Your body racked on bed of pain;
Alone you suffer, weep, and moan,
Your aches unheard, you cry in vain.

Oh woman, give that child the right
To live as God gave life to you.
He'll help you in your hour of need,
You will be happy if you do.

Sister Mary Kathryn Hyjek
St. Louis, MO

OLD COWBOY

Old cowboy tried and true
boots of black and levis of faded blue
I really didn't know you all that well
But from a great distance a real cowboy I could tell

Your work was hard the hours long
the trails were rough so you had to be strong
God, family and a horse
the things that made your everyday good and without remorse

Your son that I knew better than I knew you
Showed me a stranger his love for you
You must have been a very good man because real love is earned
not given with a grain of sand

The first time I saw you on a horse you sat
that you were a real cowboy there was no doubt
You touched my life that very day
Just an old cowboy tried and true
Boots of black and levis of faded blue

Weldon O. Isham
Graford, TX

TRIBAL

At this late-Saturday-summer-night
must-outdo-their-friends
Jewish-center wedding
the well-rehearsed
  well-costumed duo
seem to have cornered the market
on blessedness.

Chair-carried, then danced around
applauded, kissed, and tambourined
they forget when they were less
than centers of the worlds
of their resplendent guests.

Some rain-plagued autumn
a few sighs down the road
when togetherness
wed to bills, parenthood
predictability
has become their tawdry albatross
how much will they remember
how much will they believe
this gilded bliss?

Louise Jaffe
Brooklyn, NY

GATHERING DRIFTWOOD UPON APPLEDORE

Climbing a lonely ledge to watch
The sunrise upon the sea
Lying like a mirror
In the gentle island breeze

Reflecting on a childhood of tidepools
Morning glories and beach peas
And sleepy dreams surrounded by
The sounds of the sea

Learning to tend the tower lamps -
The daughter of a lighthouse keeper
Always on the edge of the foam
Dancing with the sandpipers

Listening to the slap of the waters
Against the lonely ledge
As behind distant silent sails
An indigo sun bursts from the ocean's edge

Even though time fades years
Like fresh drawing in the sands
She suddenly catches once again
An angry lobster with her hands

Knowing the cycles of seasons
As only isolation allows -
Like the final migration of the puffins -
This lighthouse flame grows pale now

Alonzo Augustus Jones
Tulsa, OK

BITTER SWEET

looking up
through dying, twisted
arthritic limbs of
the old apple tree,
once so alive, so green
bending with fruit---
for one short moment
the sharp and tangy taste
of apples comes sweet to my tongue
while a child's laughter
fades off at a distance
as the setting sun
kisses the mountain;
though years have passed
the memory lingers
and will be with me
always___________

Faye Kaestner
Louisville, KY

THE HOUSE

The house harbors
ells built one by one
  a jumble of stairways
too many rooms, too many levels
  twists and turns.
    I blunder in the maze of corridors
trying to find my room,
  the one with cushions
heaped on the fourposter.
    In one room frail granny
asleep in rumpled gown,
  gently lifted, fabric smoothed,
covered against cold,
    curls like a leaf in bud.
    Next door silent, withdrawn Annie
clutches her pillow
  sighing with longing
fantasizing a lover,
  murmuring a name.
    Alone in candlelight
mother brushes her long hair
    before the oval mirror
drawing the house around her
    like a peignoir.

Emma Landau
New York, NY

EXTRACTS FROM THE COLLECTIVE
(Extinctively Primitive)

I was feeling extinctively primitive
Sitting by a Paleozoic pool-side
Explaining to a trilobite
The taste of shrimp remoulade

It felt comforting to know
I'd made an impression
That my grey matter was in the pink
Flush in the flesh, that I could think

... That I'd be fed
Living in the energetic red
That the dominant status of my specie wasn't dead
Since necessity breeds ingenuity...

Miraculous to consider we
Had the common sense
To replace extracted crude
With a parting of the sea

Through pressurized catheters of anonymity
A transfusion replacing blood with piss
Syphoning marrow, injecting spit
... I guess I'm used to it...

The stress tolerance of thinking deeply
In instinctively intuitive analogy,
That creatures in the height of glory
Are set in the crown of endangerment...

Extinctively primitive, creative dinosaurs
Battering ourselves with inventive meteors
Flooding a strata of potential down the drain
With violence and desire unrestrained

I was thinking about the cosmos in our brain
About the starch our bio-mass contains
And the love that sustains the power
To pull it out.

Leslie Levy
Los Angeles, CA

YOU COME A DANCIN'

Do you have to be so handsome?
You are the best I've ever seen.
You know I told you not to come,
But you danced right into my dreams.

Nothing can ever work for us
Our worlds are just too far apart.
So, I'll do what's right for us,
To give each a brand new start.

When I lay me down to sleep,
I know you will surely show--
Why can't you just stop teasing me,
Why can't you just let it go.

Then you come a dancin',
A dancin' through my dreams.
You know you have that look,
The one that thrills me so--
But I can see through your schemes
So please just let me go.

You must be so sure of me,
The way you gently come and go,
So please dance away from me
Life goes on, so does the show.

Don't come a dancin',
A dancin' through my dreams
Don't tease me any more.
Why not do what is kind?
Why not let me go?

Shirley Ann Longnecker
Goshen, IN

THE CARDINAL

The heat of summer is gone,
The bare branches of trees
Dance a silhouette of restless grace.
There is wonder in this airy dance
Of a few silken leaves embracing weathered twigs.
Then out of nowhere comes the Cardinal --
Scarlet and splendid, quicker than light,
Across the hedges, winging a shining way.
A creature to warm the very heart of winter.
He has no place in this calendar of snow and ice.
He is the majesty of earth and sky and birds;
He brings a crimson joy beyond the power of words.

Florence Lonsford
New York, NY

BACK TO THE LAND

I hear the call of the bidding land
that nurtured me through the years
and paced me to the brink of man
with symmetry unspoiled by fears...

It was there in the rolling hills
that I played as a barefoot boy
and felt the touch of kindred fields
sown with many seeds of joy...

I feel the lure of the old homestead
that sheltered and patterned me
and encased for me a feather bed
quilted with dreams of infinity...

There beneath the soft blue sky
I made my covenant with earth
and still my thoughts at random fly
back to the hills of my birth...

M. Rosser Lunsford
Eatonton, GA

GUATEMALAN WEAVING

The peasant woman kneels, for months,
to weave delicate designs into
ritual power. The backstrap loom

around her buttocks steadies the rod
in her lap. Strands from it
flow up to another rod
tied to a sturdy tree.

Fifty-two sacred bands,
half a hand wide, create
a narrow cloth twice as tall
as she can stand. Arrows of green,
fushsia zig-zags, diamonds of blue--
dozens of triangled shapes
and hues form the long strip.

Here and there, she adds no color,
allows the basic woven red
to pulse instead. One band is filled
with mythic quetzals, the name for both
her money and her tribal bird.

Her faultless pledge unfolds upon
my neck, my shoulders and my breast.
Stitch by stitch, I absorb
silent grace and mystic warmth
that touch and teach my inner space.

Annette Lynch
South Pasadena, CA

REPOSE

I shall sit here
With music and thought and meditation,
With poetry and prayer.
I shall sit here forever.
They must come to me.
I shall not look--
Nor try to cope, nor figure,
  nor give my opinion
Of the thousand devilish questions
  of the well-informed,
Whose truth is but wishful illusion.
I shall not dance their tune,
Nor think their thought,
Nor say isn't that awful;
I shall sit here,
The melody of love sounds
The eternal surprise...
I shall not go
They must come for me.

John Manier
Dayton, OH

HOME AT LAST

Without your smile, life would be
Alone, adrift, and lost at sea.
Without the lighthouse of your eyes,
Darkness would pervade the skies.
Without the harbour of your heart,
Love would need a place to start.
Embracing arms, lips kiss the shore;
At home at last, forevermore.

A. V. Santa Maria
Rahway, NJ

HARD LIFE OF MORTIFICATION

The blend of solitude and communal life in
A Carthusian cloister is certainly unique.
It is of course one of the largest and clearest
Mirrors of saintly life; in one word,
The Carthusian monk is an exceptional human being.
His faith must be stronger than the iron gates
Of the prisons to struggle against all temptations;
It should be like the brightest sun
To lead him forward and shine his paths
He humbly and willingly elects to hide
And keep away from the world's vanity.
In fact, he vehemently kicks the world
With all its luxuries and pleasures.
He achieves all this at the nick of time
When he feels the inclination to embrace
Forever and ever the Carthusian Order.
The Carthusian monk regularly attends
The choir, prays and eats his meal alone
In his simple and bare cell.
There is no breakfast for the Carthusian,
But, there is neither gloom nor despair.
Only once a week and on feast days he dines
Together with his brethren in the refectory.
The big garden provides the necessary vegetables
As the Order of the Carthusian is strictly vegetarian.
He even spends his studying hours
In the library where manuscripts are well kept.
This hard life envelopes his spiritual activities
And the perfect silence he lives in.

Victor Marroun
Zejtun, Malta

THE QUICK LEARNER
(for Fiona, aged nine, at Easter)

In school, at five, I *knew* how to fly
but a friend named Bigger, bolder than I
gave me a banner to wear on my head
FLYING IS WRONG, IS WRONG, it said.

It streamed out behind me
whenever I took off
Did I know about space? Heck no. But soft!
Oh soft! I was soaring, I was soaring. I *knew* how to fly
I was roaring, I was roaring, to the sweet bye-and-bye

But I learned, then, quickly, exactly how to fall
Off-earth bouncin', like Icarus. Tall.
I learned not to fly too close to the sun
which would melt my wings and spoil all the fun

I died, then, to flying, started to be
King Kong? Ding Dong? Wild and free?
Something new? Something silly?

They gave me a nickname
Willy the Nilly

I learned how to say, in French, "Who, moi?"
They laughed and they loved me
They oo-la-la-ed.

I learned, then, to ride, Cutesy, on top
on top of the good ship
Lolli-pop.

I forgot, I forgot, I forgot about flying
I lost my friend. I took up dying
Many, many, many, many small little deaths
from which I learned, quickly, to

resurrect.

Grace B. Martin
Buffalo, NY

FRIENDS AND LOVERS

During the day they were friends,
At night they were lovers.
Just a touch of his hands would leave her spellbound.
He didn't know of the love she had for him,
She felt she could die of sadness in her heart.
She feared the day he would leave,
But she kept the secret with all her might.
She had a wall blocking her heart's desire,
He had a wall blocking the truth.
She would sit in the dark,
She would cry from depression.
All she wanted was for him to love her,
But that he plainly said he could not.
Her heart sank to her gut,
She was ashamed of herself and of her behaviors.
She would sometimes wonder,
  Was it love,
  Or just lust?
  Soon she would be vanished from his heart forever.

Kami Lee Martin
Elkhart, IN

A VOICE

A voice inside,
A woman's, strong, gentle, urgent.
Dormant for so long,
She is composed, mature, eager
    many times wiser,
Impatient to get out
To break free
To find a place in this space
That can mold and nurture.

For so long patient, humble and yielding,
She has watched and waited
Unaccompanied, unnoticed and unknown.
But now free
It's my turn she seems to say
I've been fed by the sun,
    by the rains and the snows
    loved by the moon and
Travelled with the constellations and the wind
Now I can make you my sister-friend.
You may rest at my side
As I lead and guide you
On my mission
To be free to be all I can

It's a voice that won't hear "no"
As the woman cries unceasingly
To be set free
So I can't and won't restrain
From her voice
    gentle, strong,
    patient for so long.

Louisa Martin
New York, NY

FOR STARTING A MELTING POT

Dearly Beloved: You will bring together
the choice ingredients of our land.
The only question now is whether
you will be stirring them into a brand-
new dish, novel and yet still resonant
of European flavors that combine
a dash of Catholic, Jewish, Protestant
salt and pepper with fine herbs and wine.
You start with lots of German thriftiness,
add English pride, much Irish poetry,
Welsh laughter, Polish courage under stress
topped off with native Indian dignity.
May all the loving care you will be spending
become a mix nothing can separate,
a special taste harmoniously blending
with no components keen to dominate.
If you can keep the needed fires hot,
this marriage makes a marvelous melting pot.

Anne Marx
Ft. Lauderdale, FL

THE MOON SHINES...

Delicate details -
the subtle light
and
shadow interplay.

The Moon Shines...
Constantly through
the night.

Such grace and style -
Guarding those of us
who cannot sleep;
restless in
our quest
to write poetry.

Maria Jan Matula
La Mesa, CA

DIAMONDS AND PEARLS

Some people can sparkle
Like diamonds against black,
Shining in their purpose,
Effervescent in life.

Others are like pearls
Given shape within shells,
Mysterious in form,
Yet matchless as gems.

Each holds subtle or strong
Natural inclinations,
Yet both diamonds and pearls
Are jewels, none the less.

Peggy McCray
Elyria, OH

WHEN THE MOON IS NEW...

If you touch Medusa
her serpents will wrap
themselves around you.
She soars through heaven
with giant wings gold fins.
Hundreds of snakes
crawling from her head.

Some long to be near
Medusa to hear her hissing
lisping songs forgetful.
She can suck blood from
throats coiling minds
past infinity before
they breathe again.

Joan McNerney
Oneonta, NY

DEADLY DESIGNS

Cold steel,
You have no warmth;
Your heart's a frigid mass,
Which slyly pierces living souls,
In war.

Helen M. McPhillips
Windham, NH

RECALL

Slipping,
Sliding,
I cascade
through a kaleidoscope
of time melting into yesteryear.

Once again I am six
and comforted by the
familiar.

No hands reach to
secure my free fall
And I gently land
in a volume of memories.

After resting in the familiar
and drinking the peace of
the known,-
Sated with memory
I slowly climb the
long road back
to reality.

Keith McUmber
Minneapolis, MN

SCALING THE SUMMIT

Have you ever thought that music lessons, a project or school
lessons could be like scaling a peak?

Some days you inch your way along and cover only the smallest
of increments. The surrounding territory yields little.

Other times you set off at a more rapid pace, covering much
ground and taking in adjacent scenes.

But joy abounds when the veil that masks understanding finally
falls away, with clarity and knowing filling your mind, the
necessities of scaling the summit.

Lorraine Melanson
Hawthorne, NJ

NONE ARE SO BLIND

What hope is there for those who will not look
Life in the face and strive to solve the things
That find expression there? The thought that flings
Itself within the pages of a book,
Beloved or left within a sheltered nook...
Is but the song that life forever sings,
As it goes lightly marching down the springs
Releasing song held in the ice-bound brook.

What hope is there for those who will not plumb
The depths of life, who turn and will not hear
What science has to say, and with a sneer
Meet all the wonders that must render dumb
Descriptive speech? In all the earth or seas
None of the creatures are so blind as these.

Goldie L. Morales
Novato, CA

AND THE WATER

bathtubs
and the bathwater in particular,
kings who sat in them.

So as the soap
fills in the past grunged tiles,
So does jazz pour into
stalls of convex glass
past my underarm hairs.
Not that any absurd notion
of being clean could
chromatically lift
me into a nonfloating world,
like when I held my breath underwater
as a child.
(My dizzy spells
seemed spiritual.)
Hungry for more,
mandating a hobby
that would induce satori
and gather dissimilar
elements into a then-bald chest.

And the water:
Bathtubs
and the bathwater in particular,
kings who sat in them.

Daniel M. Nester
Philadelphia, PA

CHE SERA

There will be claustrophobic times
When you must have a mountain or a sea,
Or you grow small and callous -
Your spirit undernourished in the flat,
  protected air.

There will be days of agonizing gray
When all that is not desert seems mirage.
The culprit is the poison of fatigue;
The antidote will come with fresh tomorrows.

There will be tightened round your heart
  a loneliness,
Clamped down around your mind a doubt
  of self:
Go deep into the hearts of fellow man
And find the cure.

H. F. Noyes
Politia, Greece

I. M.: REV. M. L. KING, JR.

Lead on, Great Africa!
You are Time's Noblest Song ...
You know how all began ...
Home of Primary Man ...
Great Africa, lead on !!!

I sure was Southern ...
Southern as sweetest "Corn Pone" ...
An African man, ...
Son of a Baptist Preacher, ...
And an African Princess ...

Lead on, Great Africa! ...
Where God's Own Son has trod ...
You peopled all the World,
And all the Flags unfurled ...
Great Africa! Lead on !!! ...

In Stockholm they gave
Me a prestigious Award,
The Nobel Peace Prize ...
In Memphis my award was
The Lone assassin's lead gift ...

Lead on, Great Africa !!!
Until the Prize is won ...
Until the Dream begun ...
Great Africa! Lead on !!! ...

Do not speak of my
Education, my degrees, ...
Material possessions ...
I died a Baptist Preacher
Reaching out for Freedom's Hand ...

Now you bring this world
Freedom for all of mankind ...
This means you must pray !!! ...
This means you must focus on
The Black Madonna and Child ...

Martin J. O'Malley, Jr.
Passaic, NJ

A CIRCUS IN THE TREES

So much to see,
The tiger jumping through a hoop,
A seal balancing a ball on its nose,
The bareback rider, the trapeze performer,
All this I saw and more.
A merry-go-round, the ferris wheel,
A clown, balloons, and cotton candy.
Oh what fun it is to see, "a circus in the trees."

Lola Opalenik
Erie, PA

BOSQUE LAND

Oh! Grand, majestic scenes of Bosque Land,
Seared in my brain before I was a man,
I see you 'though I'm in another land,
And fain would have you ever close at hand.
I see your rolling hills, once 'neath the sea,
Now covered only by blue canopy.
Cedars and yucca plants are all around,
With mesquite, try to grow in rocky ground.
Jack Rabbits with their long extended ears,
Apparently, we cause them little fear.
Less often we see sights of Cotton Tails,
Within easy sight of our chosen trail.
We leisurely walk past our horse corral,
Flush a long legged running chaparral.
Turkey buzzards float on the upward drafts,
Appearing as dark, death foreboding craft.
From off the hill we follow river road,
And into the river bottom we strode.
We stepped inside the long rows of cotton,
Saw small horned toads, I have not forgotten;
Then saw squirrels playing in pecan trees,
While Flicker drilled in trunks for bugs to seize.
On Mustang vines were hung tart purple grapes,
While from forest trees the vines were draped.
Sometimes my pilgrimage, I would extend,
So I could include, river's horseshoe bend.
The Grebes dove to get out of my sight.
Was a game with us, there was no real fright.
My fish lines held two yellow cat for me.
On the bank I checked giant cotton-wood trees,
That sometimes sent their fuzz upon the breeze.
When my love tour of inspection was done,
I felt with Mother Nature, we were one.
Bosque, I see, all this from memory.
I'd love once more to live within your lee.

Donald Owen
Hallettsville, TX

SPRINGTIME

Spring on the inside
can b all year round.
Just keep loving memories
close at hand
and let them bud forth
when there is danger
of frost and cold.
Spring, 1990

Bernadette Palma
Milwaukee, WI

THE UNKNOWNS
(Dedicated to all dedicated parents and teachers.)

Where is the next generation
  The women and men who would give;
They died before procreation
  Would give them their free choice to live
Knife them was then a fixation
  It was titled as new woman's lib;
We now feel the gap in creation...
  They bled that a license might sieve.

Where is the live recreation
  The teens with their laughter and joy;
Oozing with new penetration
  Excitement the tools of their ploy;
Where are their "right on" inventions
  That might have eased our employ;
We now feel their gap in creation...
  They bled that a license might sieve.

The folly of their uncreation
  Now fears all the minds that had thought;
That through a life limitation
  More space in time may be bought;
Instead of a fine infiltration
  Of ideals, unfoldeds, un-wroughts;
We now know their gap in creation...
  Babes bled that a license might live.

Libs still bleed the next generations
  They must, or lost is their lib:
World fears an over population...
  Babes bled that a license might live.

Sr. Phoebe Passler
Lacey, WA

BREAKTHROUGH

Sometimes no matter what
you say or do, it will be
maligned or misconstrued;
unresolved in one locus
breakthrough may come with
a humbler focus and
there is such hope in
small resiliences:
the abandoned tidepool
(teeming with life)
a weed (in flower no less)
in a side walk crack
and that ever-hopping
never-stopping chickadee
pecking for (and finding)
invisible morsels --
glimpses of a cosmic pattern;
there is some incomparable
mutuality between
resilience and rapport
(just wait, you'll see.)

M. Dilecta Planansky
Shaw Island, WA

NADIR'S HOPE

Food of the sea and housing of the moon
were fair prospects once, until we had
that pitherful of fervors, that wild bolt
not knowing where to hurl itself, but hurl
it must--and now the consequence foredoomed.
Cold, glassy, in a sempiternal fix
smoke settles. Figures in the aftermath
stiffen, obscenely moral, uniform;
and Satan's children reap the monument--
an immortality bestowed on rods.
The victims and conspirators are one:
they slew the spirit with solemnity
and made us guilty long before we sinned.
Tell it to them who do not wish to hear.

Mariquita Platov
Tannersville, NY

HE COMES!

O Sapientia - You spake the Word and it was done.
The earth, the seas, the heavens were made;
and man, in image of yourself; and beasts, and
  fowls, and fishes, too,

O Adonai - Lord and Healer of a people to whom
  you first revealed yourself.
To Abraham, with promise of lands and seed;
to Moses, in burning bush and with the Law, your Word.
A gradual revelation, awaiting the fullness of time.

O Radix Jesse - In the measured slowness of eternity,
  yet another sign.
Hope for peoples in despair; promise for nations,
  not yet formed;
for generations, not yet born.

O Clavis David - Free us from our prisons of pride
  and greed and hate;
Throw open wide the gate and bring us quick release.

O Oriens - Light ineffable; brighter than a host of
  stars, the total sum of suns, myriad of moons.
Enlighten the darkness of our lives, our sordid lives
  and morbid souls.
Remove the fear of the darkness of death.
Grant life everlasting in an eternity of light.

O Rex Gentium - King of all; not for one flock, contained
  in borders, hemmed in by middle sea and adjacent desert.
Sovereign of limitless domain, burst our boundaries.

O Emmanuel - God with us, not over or beyond us.
Promised before the earth was made, heavens formed;
yes, before the beginning of beginning.
Dwell with us.

O Virgo Virginium - Lowliest of women; greatest of Mothers,
  chosen to bear the Divine Mystery, to fulfill the
  Divine Promise:
The Kingdom of God and His only Begotten Son.
He comes!

Mary L. Plowe
Cincinnati, OH

SMALL JOURNEY

Today I followed
a butterfly through flowers
in my small garden.
Come again tomorrow. Please.
We lingered there too briefly.

Judith Ahrens Powell
Richland, WA

GOLDEN STATE
(Haibun)

Overnight six brushfires were set in the Golden State.
As flames reached the sky, and ash drifted on the wind,
acrid smoke stung our eyes and parched our throats. Huge
clouds of it touched the heavens, and the scent made its
home in every pore. Shifting winds, now and then, reveal-
ed the tinder on every hillside.

    a crow alights
    on a charred twig...
    its halo of smoke

Heroes were easy to find. They gathered the horses, res-
cued domestic pets, and delivered children to grateful
families. Some wild animals found their way

    out of the firestorm
    a fox and hare...
    their feral smiles

    after the firestorm
    the lingering essence
    of man's greater good

Gloria H. Procsal
Oceanside, CA

MISCELLANEOUS

the world
is beyond me.
people look around
but cannot see.
i am more than a person
for i am rare.
how can others
compare?
my time will come
and I will be **OUTRAGEOUS!**
so who are those people
who consider ME miscellaneous?

Adela Rosa Ramos
North Miami, FL

SHARDS, POTS AND DEER

Pendant shaped shards
Found on a southwest dig
Move rhythmically, clink musically
Like small coins
In my clasped hollow palms

My thoughts thread them
On an earth colored
Leather thong between soft feathers
For a decorative necklace,
Prudently my fingers fashion shards
Into a complete cooking vessel

Another woman, an indigenous one
Once hand made many
Using sticky stoney sand,
Her small daughter delights digging
From river bed in hot sun
The pots harden as if kiln fired
her acorn pounded porridge secure within

Flushed face above burl flame
Black braids tossed back
She heaps pot size portions
Sating her teen son and other Braves
Soon to stalk deer near
Their vast forest

They vision a savory venison treat
Added to tomorrow's porridge,
Putting some by for jerky,
Their chant: 'THE GREAT SPIRIT
WILL PROVIDE BOUNTIFUL DEER'
Joins beat on deer skin drum
As they depart on faint sound
Of feet clad in deer skin moccasins

Millie Raskin
Berkeley, CA

THE OUTCAST

Part black, part white
but scorned by both
grey exists in limbo,
travels in threatening clouds
announces creeping age
breaks loose in deadly storms.

Ingrid Reti
San Luis Obispo, CA

REFINEMENT REVISITED

I came to see topaz
  and silver and springtime
the sun while it's raining
  and Chivalry's Grace
I came to hear quiet
  and laughter's sweet beauty
the whisper of teardrops
  as I touch your dear face.

I came on the wings
  of a gold and white angel
direct from the land
  of a leprechaun's dream
to find one who will show me
  amid worlds quite contrary
that refinement and LOVE
  are still what they seem.

Helen C. Rhodes
Saratoga Springs, NY

BOSNIA

The brutality of sexuality
in the incomprehensibility of normality
brings to light
the adversity in the duplicity
of the morality of war
and the purity of peace.
The raping of the innocents
corrupts us all.

R. G. Rhymes
Toyonaka, Japan

A NEW BREED OF ENTREPRENEUR

Lights from the sky
have been turned off
in the inner city.
Burned-out buildings,
litter-strewn streets
are monuments
to despair.

Department stores,
specialty shops
have been replaced
by a new breed of entrepreneur--
high school drop-out kids
peddling drugs.

They sell to neighbors,
to relatives, to suburbanites--
to anybody
looking for a fix.

Gold neckchains,
high-fashioned athletic shoes,
designer jeans
mark their success.

Bullets pound the air.
A cop, a peddler,
a toddler playing tag
fall dead, fall dead.

Shirley Rodis
Coconut Creek, FL

FALLEN TREES LIKE WITCHES

The charcoal skeletal arms
of trees stretch with bough tips
embracing sunlit heaven
leaf by leaf stripping down
upon magenta and purple heather
patterning seasonal autumn carpet
as would a ring of worshippers
applauding life's renewal
deep in ancient ritual merging
divinely into the nuances
of sunbeam drawing gradually
towards nightfall's lilting wings.

Diana Kwiatkowski Rubin
Piscataway, NJ

AMERICA SO BEAUTIFUL

All things under Heaven and in the Earth...
  The Almighty Creator did surely birth!
Majestic and great is she...
  So wonderful to see and here be.
Emerging is the ripe grain.
  There is also some pain.
Righteousness will always reign.
  America with her splendor isn't plain.
Incomplete, not quite complete...
  The Lord's Church won't be beat!
Coming on so very strong...
  Surely, Jesus won't tarry long!
Amazing is God's good grace!
  For each and every race!!!

Jack W. Runyon
East Olympia, WA

ANOREXIC

She mounts the stationary bike.
Her eyes evade the mirrored wall
and slide into the azure memory of a river.
For awhile remembrance has let her forget
and once again she's sitting in the swan shaped pedalo,
her feet steadily dipping and rising.
Then, she gases upward. The sky ripples then cracks
into the emaciated reflection of herself.
In an instant her mind can distort the image
as perversely as a fun house mirror.
The reflected figure transforms -
the hollows fill like pockets, bulging,
flesh coils around the bones,
swaddling her body in the fat that jeers back at her.

Nearly fleshless fibulas stiffen
before pumping the pedals
frantically,
attempting to flee from her torment.
Her feet pound,
igniting spokes into a blur of movement.
The shrill protest of grating metal
grows louder and louder,
reverberating into the wailing call of sirens.

Jeanne Leigh Schuler
Novato, CA

THE POET'S PLACE
(It is not the places that grace men, but men the places.— Agesilaus)

Philosophical pilgrim
whose realm ranges across Himalayas
of seasons. As historian, the Parnassian
struggles to decipher hieroglyphics carved within
the caves of men's confusion, carrying still glacial
roots and Olympian memories in an age contorted by shaven
skulls, mushroom clouds and Gulag Archipelagos. Beneath
ever shrinking dwarf stars, the doctor of words is left
to ponder the puzzles of how to erase dominions of
darkness, unlock unborn rhythms caught in
Caribbean conch shells, strip naked the
dogmas of hate, and salvage the snow
leopards from the fate of the
unicorn. As prophet, he
must lead the masses out
of the Minotaur's maze,
weave the divine around
edges of the holocaust
and challenge
false gods
stretching
to infinity.
From chaotic
storm-black
nights, he is
left to create
fragile
legends.
Seer walking
the circle
of time,
he becomes
the ancestor of truth.

Ruth Wildes Schuler
Novato, CA

COMPUTER FEAR

Surely,
it can't be
that this monstrosity
upon my desk
makes me cower so in fear?
That it could be
far smarter than I am?
That knowledge stored
within its microchips
is more than what
is stored in all
the brain cells
in my head?

Surely,
I can upstage
that box which beeps
to call attention
to mistakes
it thinks I've made.

I'll just program its
disintegration
when it executes
one more command.
If only it does not
question--or disregard--
those instructions.

Deloris Selinsky
Shavertown, PA

Edia Thaxter (1835-1894)

LIFE BEGINS AT EIGHTY

They say "Life begins at Forty."
With that I don't agree.
Because I find that I myself,
Since I've reached the eighty mark this year,
I feel more efficient and relaxed, too.
Maybe I've slowed down, finding
I do less and less and
It takes longer to do.
Nevertheless, there is a satisfaction in
Knowing there is no need to worry or fret,
If we place all our trust in God and yet,
We can take things in stride,
Cope with stress and still be happy beside!

Martha Serfozo
Erie, PA

MOTHER

She gives life to the earth.
She was there at our births.
She held us and hugged us.
She kissed us and loved us.
She comforted us in times of sorrow.
She always told us to look for a better tomorrow.
She laughed with us and helped us with our homework.
She scolded us when we were bad.
She still loved us even when she was mad.
She's always there at our side.
When we find we need a place to hide.
She confides in us and encourages us to reach for our dreams.
We follow her advice in order to live a better life.
The life of wisdom and education.
The life of much happiness and growth.
Our mother, the guide in our lives, the teacher, the aid, the farmer, the mourner, the
wise one, the one who loves us unconditionally.

Stephanie Sinclair
Louisville, KY

ON BEING A WOMAN
("To be is precisely to fulfil or to give warrant to ideas by making possible
the experience that the ideas define"--Josiah Royce

It takes time. First the idea and then
some guesses at the truth about us.
We but slenderly know ourselves, establish
little systems on buried stilts, like Venice.
Yes, women are like Venice--full of canals
and bridges to the world, shrouded in
a mystery of strange effects
because of interior tides.

Integrating sting and honey,
we tend to bind compulsions
with cold philosophy.

Scars of time and childbirth strain
the patterns, which change with age,
regrouping at each turning,
and yet the center holds when we are lucky.
Inwardness protects us from the world,
from little things afflicting us.

We are ourselves and others down the streets
of neighborhoods and history--our job to nurse
the world, to construe its actions and feel
within our bones the instincts of a woman.

It's an unsentimental journey,
this balance between nothing and being a woman,
until we're stung into being by
circumstance.

Mary Wren Small
Wilmette, IL

ARCHIVES

Archives could tell you all that is has been.
Before your time, you lived. You live again.
Your spears and arrowheads, your guns and swords
unearth you equally as Shakespeare's words
and Parliamentary parchments set on shelves
exhibit lively aspects of our selves.
Continuum runs stranded through the race:
whose molecules, whose dust does mine embrace?
An archive lives within, and I have been,
infrequently, in search of ghosts of me
whose wails and laughter generate a life
that clears and unifies, is mine not quite
entirely. I'm welded with the world
which shares its ancient bowls and spoons with God.

Wilma Spellman
Park Ridge, IL

CHILDHOOD MAGIC

I held the stars aloft in trembling sun
  and watched them dance and glisten bright-
I heard the roar of ocean in a shell
  and felt the heartbeat of the pulsing tide.
I rode the wings of thrush through cloudless skies
  and dreamed in peace on mountain peaks below-
I crept with ladybug up emerald blade
  and spun a web with spider on the eaves.
I opened rosebud at the dawn
  and found therein a mite, a sandgrain small-
I chased a silver minnow in a creek;
  pursued a turtle 'neath the shadowed bridge.
I blushed with oak leaves, kissed by autumn wind
  and joined the geese in wild serenade-
I celebrated birthdays with delight
  and feast-times all too far between.

Then, alas, I found I had grown up
  and cast aside the foolishness of youth-
Exchanged my fun for serious pursuit,
  my glee for self-consuming tasks.
Until, one day, I watched an infant play
  and found my own soul, oh, so gently call-
"Release me! Unlock my prison door!"
  And, so, with great relief,
  I shed what was not real
  and rediscovered long-lost secret key
  to childhood magic-
    forgotten
  in the heart of me!

Sr. Ann Stamm
Livonia, MI

CHERRY-BLOSSOM WINE
(To Marla Schoen)

Past my dripping, bedroom window
the cherry bough is drenched
with cherry blooms in charcoal mist.

An armour-plated cocoon
blossoms a Viceroy butterfly
in swirl of cherry petals and misting wind.

Cloudbanks sway in cherry boughs
clotted with Viceroy butterflys
and the sifting down of cherry petal wing-tips.

The bursting out
of these cherry blossoms, Marla,
...and when will I see your face at my door, again?

Richard Stepsay
Denver, CO

THE GIFT

I think to know my Father,
His gifts when I receive,
Does smile from where He sits
To watch my countenance.

As though upon His knee,
The child in me assents
To take the bright red ribbon off
To let the play commence.

What mortal parent greater
Sees the joy at hand
When Inspiration gathers
To the dance unplanned.

Linda J. Stewart
Prince Edward Island, Canada

MORN'S EARLY AIR

Bone chilling cold, its dawn erupts,
The days orange fingers stretching up,
The waiting calm of winters morn,
Forgotten was the chill of last night's storm.

And now silent stillness in morn's early air,
Unleashed was winter's tiger from his lair,
The numbness of the dawn escapes the night
Revealing the icy clutch of frost, stark and bright.

The frost, clinging like magnet to branch and vine,
Etched was the silver thread with icy climb,
Breath came then painfully to me
As merciless cold grasped at hand and knee.

Breath froze midway through frosty air,
Making all Nature stop and stare,
Thus awake once more to old winter's cloak,
That this was winter's story wrote.

I drew my coat tighter at the throat,
And faced the blast of the icy note,
While smiling silently to myself at last
I knew winter's story had come to pass.

Robert Stirling
Nova Scotia, Canada

IN LOVING MEMORY OF JANE C. WELCH
(Died March 3, 1994)

The vault of time slammed
Capturing you that day
Sealing and encasing
Stealing you away.

Death the last enemy
Who'll defeat you?
I hope I'm there watching
Whenever they do!

Time, STOP, reverse
Let me see her again
Open up the doors
Please let me in!

Where is the Hero?
The one dressed in white
Why was He gone?
Absent that night.

How long will the Earth
Drink mankind's blood?
Drunk with our loved ones
In it's belly of mud.

When will this pain
Cease and desist?
When death the Last Enemy
Drowns in the Abyss!

Narda R. Strong
Churubusco, IN

WHO I AM

My ancestors keep popping up everywhere
though long dead and crumbled to
dust

    Great great grandmother
    sitting in the back of the church
    her back to the minister
    the congregation a religion
    that does not know
    what her people knew always God
    is everywhere the trees the rocks
    the water the people not just in
    some building on Sundays.

    Great grandmother
    her arms folded across her chest
    her chest thrust forward daring
    anyone to oppose her matriarchal power
    question her wisdom earned trials
    by winter storms and hens whose feathers
    must be plucked one by one so much
    patience must be learned and I
    learn to fold my arms and stand firm
    too.

    Grandmother who endured
    the slights and insults of fortunes
    so outrageous
    (men of impecunious background and grandiose egos)
    she took warm comfort
    in the bosom of her family arms open
    wide always, for others ..
    whom I am.

Conciere Taylor
Flushing, NY

THE BLANKET ON THE GROUND

Picnic time it never failed to see
A patch quilt, beneath a tree
Children sleeping old men napping
babies feeding couples meeting
whatever the need
the blanket was there
to remind us we had
a home somewhere
it stood for comfort warmth security
in town or country
no matter where
I was at home with
the blanket on the ground

Josephine Copenhaver Thomas
Prescott, AZ

CHARLEMAGNE IN AIX

From Frisia to Lombardy the legend grows;
   Charlemagne cannot die.
Yet here I lie in nights consumed with sleepless struggles
   yet to breathe; I hardly dream, but seem to see.
There are fever haunted worlds, great abysses
   that endure and empty even all my pains.

Where have my children gone?

With others they turn from me, with contempt for me, not caring
   if I live or die; useless to them now.
From tropic isles I sent for them to join their mother whom I
   had won. Camille! I am with you yet my beloved;
even so you have passed through the caverns to the land above.

Shrieking shadows now wait behind.

My daughters! I showed you elk,
   and we played in new fallen snow.
Cascading forms...There...my castle vault ignites.
   Behold the firmament; torn splendid sky.
He comes once more in mail and steel.

Gabriel! Your pipers keen.

On steed of thunder—earth shaking—I would kneel.
   The king of Ind suffers havoc before the infidel.
Squire! Help me rise. Blow now my horn of hunt and war.
   Remember Roland; burst your very temples; quake these vaults
to rouse my lads. Then bring my mighty battle mount.

My knights will fear and love me once again.

I bring them holy war.

Tony Thomas
Alameda, CA

NEXT TIME MAYBE

From experience with kids
you learn that sometimes it's
better just to jump back
let it happen.

Other times you figure
you'd better put a tape over your mouth
say nothing. You say it anyway.
Three years later the kid says
you said such and such.

"No, you must have dreamt it."

A summer my brother was nineteen
he fell in love with the girl in the next
cottage. Walls upstairs were a way from the
ceiling and I overheard my parents say they
didn't like her but the worst thing
would be to say so.

Next day my brother said at supper he'd spent
half the summer's earnings on a radio
for her grandmother. *"A radio for her grandmother!"*
MY MOTHER SHRIEKED.
Out of the bag, clearly,
that was
then.

Ellen Tifft
Elmira, NY

THE GIFTS

Your father found another home.
You knew he would
when you looked through a window,
thinking it was a dream or mirror,
and saw his shadow laughing with others
who had already become real to that place.
His parting gift to you:
the tears wrapped within yourself,
to be taken out and used when needed.
Your no-longer need of them
will be your housewarming gift to him.

Patricia Ann Treat
Bremerton, WA

HELLO, GOD!

Hello, God, it's me again. I know I've been away;
I meant to come back sooner, but I didn't know what to say.
And then I met a friend of yours who asked me if I knew
that every good thing in my life is all because of You!
Why is it that we blame You -- if I may be so bold?
When things don't go the way we want, it's You, God, that we scold,
A bountiful garden to live in, and yet from You we stray,
and how ashamed I am that I had nothing to say.
Did I thank you for the snowfall, or the beauty of the sun?
Or the splendor of a sunset as another day is done?
Did I thank you that I 'wakened and could stand upon my feet?
And, oh yes, that I've an appetite and plenty of food to eat?
While all the gifts in nature bring us pleasure and happiness,
We forget that your hand formed us in your very own image and likeness.
And so, dear God, I'm sorry that my love I did not show,
But I promise from now on that I will stop to say "Hello."

Patricia Truscello
Tewksbury, MA

DO YOU KNOW WHAT TOMORROW IS?

it is the eve of the anniversary date
I am standing at the sink
slicing strawberries
seeing his blue eyes
remembering
how with one leg crossed over the other
he stood listening to the radio
how he helped with the dishes
and homework
introduced me to Cinderella
at Radio City
laughed when an ungrateful monkey
spit peanuts back at him
at Central Park Zoo
how we glided as though
we were Fred and Ginger
at my cousin's wedding
how he never danced at mine
played with his grandchildren
or read even one of my poems--

the telephone rings
cutting memory
my mother, reminding,

"Do you know what tomorrow is?"

Sonia Usatch
Brookhaven, NY

THE PEACOCK
("The pride of the peacock is the glory of GOD." — Wm. Blake)

The beauty and charm of the peacock
maddens me when my eyes catch this unique bird
whose pride is *the glory of God.*

I look at him with wonder. His charms
do not fail me to know the presence of God.
His attractive colors make me
think over undying human sufferings
that are not found in him. Whether
he is conscious of his charms or not,
he is a poet's joy forever.

He dances in the rainy season
when clouds comfort him from the sun's
tyranny. If rain does not fall in time
he prays to god, Indra, for rainfall.
His chanting words echo the sky at daybreak.
While mortal ears deaf to hear his prayer
that breaks my sleep and
fills my heart with divine emotions.

When the prayer is accepted and the
clouds float, he, then, dances
in poetic ecstasy, fanning his feathers
like a lady's fan. As soon
as he sees me he stops
his dance suddenly like a coy girl and,
then, struts into the bushes leaving
me in a deserted and tyrannical world.

Y. N. Vaish
Aligarh City, India

KATE, A SONG FOR YOUR LOVE

Give me white sands or gray rocks or pink shells,
Jade pines, saw grass or bare dunes,
Give me a mansion on top of a bluff
Where the sea song's a muted tune;

Or a shanty that's perched at the edge of the tide
So that waves storm up to the door.
A dory, the beach, the arch of sky,
The sound of the surf on the shore.

Give me the horn's duet with the fog,
A bell, jangling warnings of shoals.
Give me the sounds of the sea for my bride
And the ocean's kiss for my soul.

And the city's strain and vexations;
And the petty cares that prey
Dissolve in the salt scented darkness,
Disappear in the mists of the day.

Howard Van Dine
Bristol, VT

LAST ONE

Last one left, all
the others have disappeared
because of the weather.

Struggling to survive,
no longer red, but
a faded pink.

Wind blows the blossoms,
as petals dance
freely in the wind.

Stripped
from the stem
floating away,

not to be
seen, until
next spring.

Jim Ward
Louisville, KY

SOLITUDE

It was dawn and the rising sun
spread its carpet of amber hues
across the waves rolling in slow swells.
The song of the surf merged with
the mating call of sandpipers,
the honking of geese headed north,
the cry of gulls across the water.

She sat quietly watching the sunlight
slice through the clouds over the
high brown cliffs towering above
the rocks below.
She knew there was hatred, injustice, bigotry
in the world, but she never let them consume her.
She always lived life on the tiptoe of expectancy,
a great adventure in which no chapter should be missed.

When life tried to intimidate her,
she found healing communing with God
in the quietness of woods and fields,
the wild glory of birds and flowers,
but the sea was her first love, the sea.

E. Marie Woerner
Lincoln, NE

FOR CENTURIES...

For centuries
I have waited for this birth
The Messiah
The King among kings
He has captured and reigned
In my heart
And soul
I pay homage to Him
He the most high
Desperately
I protect Him
From those who lack understanding
They are fools
Who do not realize the great importance
I wait in silence
In His honor
Without reward or promise
I would sacrifice my self so that
He may live eternally
Yet
He lives for another

Laureen Wong
San Francisco, CA

OUTSIDE THE CROOKED TWINE CIRCLE

When conversation spins easy
as greased ball bearings
and the digits grow red whiskers
she flicks a live butt
in my Mason jar of red wine
to say she will stay.
After her breathing gets naked
she sits bolt upright
like a child claiming monsters,
"I am a marble
of aqua blue and seaweed green
that chooses to live
outside the crooked twine circle."

Sometimes when the conversation spins
like greased ball bearings
and the digits grow red whiskers
she asks to stay the night.
After her breathing undresses
she pleads with her hands
like a child needing water,
"I am so lonely."

Brian R. Young
Elkhart, IN

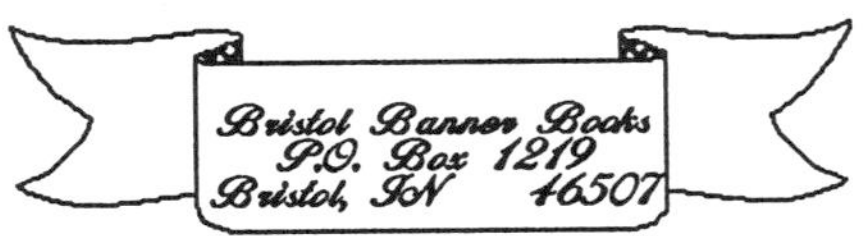

AN EDITORIAL NOTE

Every year an Editorial Advisory Board is selected to include eight international literary figures from the major learning centers of the English-Speaking world -- The University College of Wales, Cambridge University, Oxford University, The University of Sidney, Rhodes University, King's College (USA), Dalhousie University of Halifax, and The University of Edinburgh. Our goal is excellence and our ambition is to bring before the English-speaking public new and fresh poetic talent. All of this is by way of indicating a serious and enduring commitment to excellence in literature and survival in business. All titles which receive a contract to publish must carry a subvention underwrite. We publish about one manuscript out of every eight submitted. Our art department creates excellent design. Our manufacturers produce a beautiful book. We follow with an aggressive marketing campaign.

If you would like to receive a descriptive brochure on this Bristol Banner Books poetry series along with a gift copy of a recently released title, simply return the order form below. The book and brochure are free and there are no obligations. Please do not submit a manuscript without first reading the brochure which includes manuscript submission specifications.

➤ POETS WANTED ◄

To receive information on how to enter our anthologies, simply return the order form below.

(cut along dotted line)

Please check one:

______ descriptive brochure, ______ poets wanted, ______ if you would like both.

Send to address given below:

____
(Please print name here clearly)

____
(Please print address/apartment number here)

____
(Please print city/state/zip here)

Send order to: **"ORDER FORM"**
Bristol Banner Books
P.O. Box 1219
Bristol, IN   46507

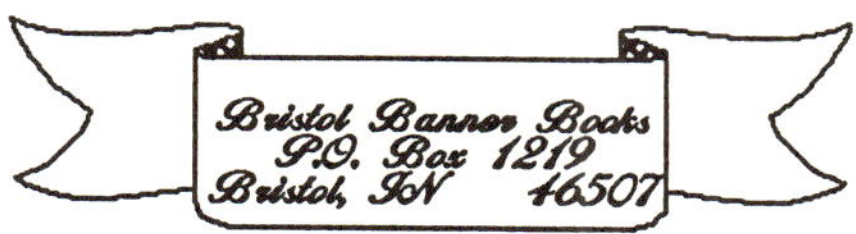

AN EDITORIAL NOTE

Every year an Editorial Advisory Board is selected to include eight international literary figures from the major learning centers of the English-Speaking world — The University College of Wales, Cambridge University, Oxford University, The University of Sidney, Rhodes University, King's College (USA), Dalhousie University of Halifax, and The University of Edinburgh. Our goal is excellence and our ambition is to bring before the English-speaking public new and fresh poetic talent. All of this is by way of indicating a serious and enduring commitment to excellence in literature and survival in business. All titles which receive a contract to publish must carry a subvention underwrite. We publish about one manuscript out of every eight submitted. Our art department creates excellent design. Our manufacturers produce a beautiful book. We follow with an aggressive marketing campaign.

If you would like to receive a descriptive brochure on this Bristol Banner Books poetry series along with a gift copy of a recently released title, simply return the order form below. The book and brochure are free and there are no obligations. Please do not submit a manuscript without first reading the brochure which includes manuscript submission specifications.

➤ POETS WANTED ◄

To receive information on how to enter our anthologies, simply return the order form below.

(cut along dotted line)

Please check one:

______ descriptive brochure, ______ poets wanted, ______ if you would like both.

Send to address given below:

____
(Please print name here clearly)

____
(Please print address/apartment number here)

____
(Please print city/state/zip here)

Send order to: **"ORDER FORM"**
Bristol Banner Books
P.O. Box 1219
Bristol, IN   46507

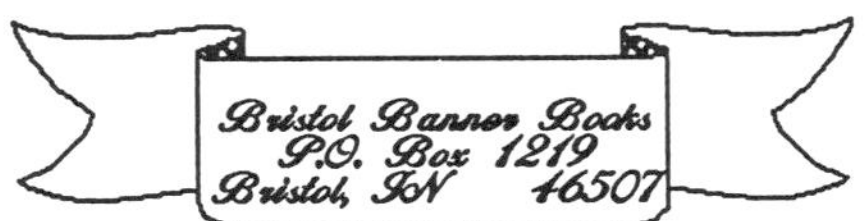

AN EDITORIAL NOTE

Every year an Editorial Advisory Board is selected to include eight international literary figures from the major learning centers of the English-Speaking world — The University College of Wales, Cambridge University, Oxford University, The University of Sidney, Rhodes University, King's College (USA), Dalhousie University of Halifax, and The University of Edinburgh. Our goal is excellence and our ambition is to bring before the English-speaking public new and fresh poetic talent. All of this is by way of indicating a serious and enduring commitment to excellence in literature and survival in business. All titles which receive a contract to publish must carry a subvention underwrite. We publish about one manuscript out of every eight submitted. Our art department creates excellent design. Our manufacturers produce a beautiful book. We follow with an aggressive marketing campaign.

If you would like to receive a descriptive brochure on this Bristol Banner Books poetry series along with a gift copy of a recently released title, simply return the order form below. The book and brochure are free and there are no obligations. Please do not submit a manuscript without first reading the brochure which includes manuscript submission specifications.

➤ POETS WANTED ◄

To receive information on how to enter our anthologies, simply return the order form below.

(cut along dotted line)

Please check one:

______ descriptive brochure, ______ poets wanted, ______ if you would like both.

Send to address given below:

____
(Please print name here clearly)

____
(Please print address/apartment number here)

____
(Please print city/state/zip here)

Send order to: "ORDER FORM"
                            Bristol Banner Books
                            P.O. Box 1219
                            Bristol, IN   46507